Earthly To Ethereal

Thoughts While Relaxing on a Costa Rican Hot Tin Roof

Peter J. Esseff

Design & Graphics
Mary Sullivan Esseff

EARTHLY TO ETHEREAL

Published in the United States by ESF Publishing, a division of Educational Systems for the Future, Inc., Tampa, FL.

Printed by CreateSpace, a DBA of On-Demand Publishing, LLC.

ESF Publishing books may be ordered through online booksellers or by contacting:

ESF Publishing
11415 Georgetown Circle
Tampa, FL 33635
813.814.1192

Thanks to the following sites for providing the fabulous copyright-free graphics: pixabay.com, bravenet.com, google.com. There is no intention to use copyrighted images illegally. If we inadvertently used one, please notify us and we will correct it.

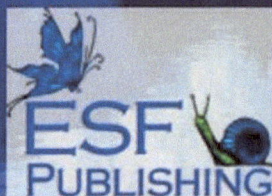

CONTENTS

The Shell of a Nautilus Snail represents the magical Fibonacci Numbers and the Golden Ratio.

DEDICATION

I wish to dedicate my book to
my loving, beautiful, talented wife,
Mary,
who spent countless hours
creating the most exquisite
photo illustrations for
each and every poem of this collection.

The photos she gathered
surround the poems and
give them a new life.
Each page speaks to the viewer
in a way that no print-only work
– no matter how inspiring – can.

Her work is a tribute to her creative genius.
There are no words that can express
my deepest gratitude for what
she has accomplished.

I love you, my darling wife.

NEW FRIENDS

DENTAL CLINIC

This week
I met four couples
and one young man;

we lived under the same roof
in a dental clinic in Costa Rica.

They all hailed
from the US:
Florida, California,
North Carolina, Texas,
New York and Alaska.

All are sporting
brand new teeth,
but not the disposable kind.

My wife
has new teeth too.

I'm the only person
In residence
who can say:
I have all my
old teeth.

I don't mind, since
I'm the only one
who doesn't have
to take pain pills.

MIRACLES

Time swept
into time
past into present,
present into past
past into future.

My mind sees
what my heart embraces
unknown into unknown.

Desire fuels my wishes;
my wishes lean
upon my cares
and turns them
into reality.

Sounds escape
the warm air
and lays them
gently on
foreign rooftops,
where voices
singe the Spring air.

Cell towers
listen to bells
calling me
to prayers.

Symmetry

What do a bird,
a cat, a fly,
a garden leaf and I
have in common?

God created us all.

Also, God's hand
makes each of us
perfect.
we all magnify
our Creator.

Also, the cat preens;
the bird flies
where it will;
the fly and leaf just are;
and I give God glory.

Without me, leaf,
fly, bird,
and cat,
the earth is a far less
happy place.

Thank you God,
for the cat,
the bird,
the fly,
the leaf,
and me.

3

Nature Is No Mother

Nature gives us life and at the same time takes it away; ancient people called Nature god.

The God we know gave us dominion over the earth, yet made us subject to nature.

No matter how hard we try to conquer it, nature ever triumphs; in a single moment, nature mocks our vanity.

Death and Life lie in its path, as Nature deceives us, posing as mother with no motherly instincts.

4

Fear the false mother, all you unwise mortals.

SILENT EXPECTATIONS

A dead leaf
bounces along
a corrugated metal rooftop,
guided only
by a covered electric wire.

The leaf
flutters and moves
only at the mercy
of the wind,
its course guided
by an eternity
of moments.

My life, like the leaf,
moves as well,
guided by an eternity
of loving moments.

My destiny,
unlike the leaf,
changes directions
from eternal moment,
to eternal moment
arriving at last
to its final destination.

Cars and trucks
move endlessly
along narrow streets
carrying life forms
in perpetual motion

Horns blare;
tires screech;
whistles blow
and sirens wail,
as life moves forward
and backward,
going nowhere.

One small city
in one small land,
at one small moment
of endless time,
cut short by living
and dying.

Voices heard in timeless motion,
going nowhere,
but being somewhere,
unknown to billions yet unborn,
Who live silent expectations.

5

TALKING

The Apostle James says more sins are committed by the tongue than any other part of the body.

God talks and I hear, but do not listen; I talk but God listens to my every word.

God tells me to love my neighbor; and I curse the driver who cuts in front of me.

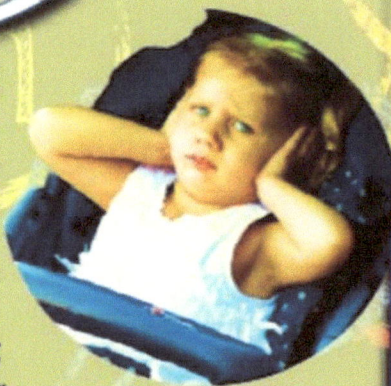

God tells me to love my enemies; and I go to great length to plan my revenge.

God tells me to turn the other cheek and my knee-jerk reaction is to strike back harder.

God, help me to listen and speak words of love and compassion.

LISTENING

Hearing is not the same as listening; mostly I hear, but rarely do I listen.

Listening is an art requiring skills, practice and determination.

Hearing comes naturally; listening comes only after years of practice.

Listening requires loving the person to whom you wish to listen.

Hearing rarely hurts; listening can engender hate, or foster deep love.

7

WALKING

Jesus walked upon the earth. He did not ride an animal except once.

He rode when He entered Jerusalem to begin His Passion and death.

Jesus walked to visit His friends. He walked to attend a wedding.

Jesus walked up mountains, and down into villages, and to shores of seas.

Jesus walked along with His disciples after He rose from the dead, after walking away from His grave.

Jesus walks with me and shares each step along the way.

8

SOUNDS

Noises litter the air
falling strangely
upon deaf ears.

No one listens
or seems to care
why or when
or from where
they emanate.

Aliens must wonder;
angels must smile;
other worlds must laugh
at such noises
made by men
the world over.

Harmless you say;
needless to contemplate;
useless to ponder;
meaningless, I think not.

These sounds
are full of mystery,
waiting to be unraveled.

Stories abound
in their strangeness,
tales of deepest meaning.
telling of tragedies,
passion and utmost joy.

9

SILENCE

Stillness comes
only from within;
there is no quiet
anywhere on earth.

Even the remotest desert,
or the furthest arctic field
knows no silence.

You and I, however,
can know quiet
even midst the cacophony
of earthly noise.

We alone,
deep in silence
of our innermost being
know, taste, feel,
and touch
the silence
that brings us
to know
who we really are.

Be silent then,
my soul, mind, spirit,
heart, and being,
and revel in
the quiet of yourself.

10

Quiet

The soul needs Quiet
to contemplate and
enter into itself,
to find the deepest spot
where God dwells.

Once found and recognized,
it's a simple task
to find Him in others.

Quiet is a sunken treasure
which can only be found
by searching the depths
of one's soul.

You need a master teacher
and much practice
until you can fathom the depths
without drowning.

The search is always a risk.
But, when you have found Quiet,
you will have found yourself in God.

11

Resting

All of me needs rest. Resting is not easy; shutting out cares and worries takes prayer and meditation.

Only God can teach me to rest, and listen to His voice and the voices of others.

Rest needs listening to hear Him and them speaking softly, quietly, gently, in touch with my heart and soul.

How sweet His voice and the voices of others inside me, joyfully singing melodies, restfulness. and peace.

SLEEPING

Scientists tell me
sleep regenerates
my body's cells.

In the realm
of the Holy Breath
sleep recreates my soul.

My soul never sleeps,
only rests
in the Holy Breath.

The Holy Breath
never sleeps.
It uses rest
to strengthen my soul.

In sleep
the Holy Breath
feeds my mind, body
and soul.

I awake from sleep
renewed
in the Holy Breath.

In sleep,
my heart
and soul
recreate
themselves
in God.

13

Dying

ying is not death;
it is, rather, coming to Life.
Without dying, there is no life.

Life is only
the after-thought
of dying.

Dying brings new Life:
the only life
worth living.

Dying brings joy,
an entrance
into time-less Life.

Dying is
life
as it should be lived.

Dying to self
moves us
into forever-living.

In dying
we share Life
with those we loved.

In dying, we love
a brand new life,
lived eternally.

Dying is
my closest friend,
making a path
to Life.

14

The Gift

A gift given
a thousand times
a second:

breath upon breath,
sending lifeblood
to muscles and bones,
ligaments and tendons,
nerves, arteries,
veins and capillaries.

Birds sing out
as men pound nails
in unharmonious syncope,
building wood and steel
into human dwelling places.

Cries of birds and
sounds of men working
compete
with cars, trucks,
and screeching brakes
for men's hearts
and minds
and souls.

A far off universe
listens
and wonders why.

15

GOD'S LOVE

If there is a God, and I firmly believe there is:

the God of my belief is infinite.

My God possesses infinite qualities, attributes, virtues, and power; my God cannot be otherwise.

When it comes to love, my God loves infinitely.

There is no greater love than the love my God has for me.

I am loved with an infinite love; my God's love for me has no bounds, is limitless and timeless.

My God is infinite LOVE.

16

Memory

Experts tell me
each millisecond of
my existence
imprints itself
on my subconscious mind.

Even in my mother's womb
I heard, felt, touched
and sensed;
nothing ever escapes
some level of my
consciousness.

Older in years,
I carry a lifetime
of sensory feelings
deep within me.

I am a living history
of millions and millions
of thoughts,
sensations and feelings,
known only to me.

Computers yet
to be discovered
cannot contain
the universe of
knowledge in me
waiting to be
discovered.

17

BOUND BY TRUST

BELIEVE IN YOURSELF

Why am I quick to say
I trust in God?
Simple to believe
but near impossible to live.

Why do I
not trust the Infinite?
Easy to ask,
but near impossible
to answer.

Why do I
not live in peace?
Easy to contemplate
but near impossible
to find.

Why do I
not love myself?
Easy to wish for
but near impossible
to attain.

Answer me, my soul.

The air bears only
a silent response,
fearing to hear
what answer cries out.

18

WINTER'S AWAKENING

A hand moves in a downward path
and silence follows
as night follows day.

Light breaks on wet timber
and cold creeps
on a gray cloud.

Summer sadly leaves me
and Autumn enters silently
precursor of a Winter's chill.

Fires light themselves quickly
and warm me in the dark
of my night souls.

I mourn the loss of a Summer's day
and fear the chill
of a Winter's night.

Sunsets spread fire
across a day-lit sky
helping me to forget
the warmth of the sun.

The earth speaks a
message of rest,
commanding me to sleep
and renew my strength.

Birds huddle and
earth responds
by sharing its stores of
harvested food
for barren nights.

Leaves die in a
burst of color
and fall to the earth,
a burial shroud for the grass.

The firs stand sentinel,
awaiting the coming
of blankets of snow.

19

THE POLE

I wonder who
first invented the pole?

The pole is everywhere:
It stands along our streets;
it hides under our roofs;
it peeks out
between houses.

Everywhere I look
I see a pole;
why did it take so long
for me to notice
the pole?

What use
is the ubiquitous pole?
Some poles are wood;
some are made of metal;
some are plastic.

Poles can do almost anything!
Is there anything a pole cannot do?
Some poles hold up buildings;
but I don't believe
metal poles can swim.

You can use a pole to jump
high in the air;
you can throw a pole great distances.

How many poles did you see today?

ROD
RENTAL
&
BAIT

20

Costa Rican Smiles

Nearly everyone smiles in in Costa Rica.

Americans flock to Costa Rica to get new teeth, simply unaffordable in the US!

Is it because new teeth cost so little, or are all Costa Ricans simply this friendly?

21

MOMENTS

Moments are for living,
awake or sleeping;
moments touch me,
cover me, fill me
with joyful cadences.

How sweet
each moment
is to taste.

Thank you,
Father, Son and Holy Breath
for filling each moment
with such joy and happiness.

I live
each moment
in timeless joy,
knowing only
this moment
in time.

Moments are for living;
moments never die;
they live
on forever,
where they
follow me
to eternal bliss.

22

MORNING

Morning is
a harbinger of life,
a fresh start,
a new moment
entering the present;

forgetting the past,
leaving behind
mistakes,
failures,
falls and tears.

Morning makes
everything possible:
brand new,
no regrets,
no looking back,
only forward,
a new start,
refreshed.

The present
is before me,
surrounds me,
fills me
with hope
and new-learned
expectations.

Seize the morning;
taste it;
relish it,
joy-filled.

THE SOUL REMEMBERS

Rain falls gently
on a wooden deck
whose boards strained
to catch and hold the drops.

So too my mind strives in vain
to catch and hold the truths falling
from the skies of some untold universe.

Frustration rises as a heron in autumn
seeking warmer climates than before,
finding companions along the way.

Innate memories hold sway
like a perpetual clock
reminding me to turn back.

My heart beats
to a never-ending rhythm
calling forth recollections of times past;
and when I do remember, all is not lost;
memories serve to enliven in me
a once dead soul.

The vision enthralls and
scares me at the same time.
It leaves me breathless
at a time when
all seems lost.

Once again,
the child in me
emerges to teach
the lessons learned
when I was young
when the earth
was old.

24

CROSS BEARER

The Cross is a symbol
and a reality.
It symbolizes death.
The reality is life.

The paradox is simple:
to die is to live;
for in living,
I embrace death,
or else it embraces me.

Some are born to the cross.
Some are dragged
kicking and screaming,
embracing it reluctantly.

Some - like me -
come to realize
there is no escaping
its loving embrace,
as I stretch out my arms,
reluctantly still.

25

CARIBBEAN CARES

Waves wash quietly
onto the Caribbean sand
while naked bodies frolic
beneath the cloud-soaked sun.

Fat bellies, sagging breasts,
and white folds of bare skin
plead with the sun to turn them brown
without pain or suffering.

For me the skin I was born with
is a timeworn burden, an inheritance
taxed away for lack of care
for my brothers and sisters in the flesh.

For me,
lines blur
between fantasy
and reality.

26

Loss

Loss is like a bridge.
If you choose to cross,
you reach a new place
in time.

Nothing is ever the same
on the other side
of the bridge.

If you fear the crossing,
you remain mired
in the loss.

Leaving the loss behind
reaching the other side
changes your life forever.

On the other side
of the bridge of loss—
there, surprises
await you.

There, you find
mothers and fathers,
sisters, brothers.

Cross the bridge,
and rejoice
in your new-
found life.

27

Clouds

As seen from below,
mountaintops
hide themselves
beneath dust-white clouds.

As seen from above,
mountain-like clouds
caress the peaks
hiding them from sight.

Lovers act like clouds,
hiding and revealing
their love
all at the same time.

Love is never one-sided,
its peaks ever open
to sunlight and the sky;
while Mystery, rather,
remains its name.

To love one another
needs both:
loving moments of hiding and
loving moments of revealing.

28

A Search For Eternity

Seagulls light upon a breakstone
hurrying to catch and dive,
crying out
impervious to my ever-
present noise.

Generations of seagulls live
in ignorance
of man's torments
and inhumanities to man.

Seagulls' cries are forever
on the vast shores
of my unconsciousness.

Human voices grate and die
of varicose veins
and week hearts.

But seagulls live on
along the shores of my yearning
for eternity.

An ocean lies at my feet
held apart from me
by a wall of monstrous stones.

Like a seductive lover,
the ocean beckons me revealing herself
naked in all her wondrous beauty.

"Enter me", she whispers,
"partake of your pleasure.
you will rest in me forever."

I stare, voyeur-like
at her beauty,
scarcely able to resist.

At the last moment,
cowardly, I turn,
afraid, and unable
to enter her depths.

Maybe, one day,
soon…

THE CHRIST CHILD

Death in Iraq, Afghanistan, Aleppo,
death in fires and drowning in floods
fill my senses with foreboding
and tell of the end of time.

Christmas is coming, harbinger of joy
when little children's smiles
fill the sky with a renewed hope.
I pray that they will see peace in their day.

Is peace too much to hope for?
What will children say when they awake one day
and find the world they've inherited
can even destroy the mind?

Dreams vie with each other
for dominance of our topsy-turvy world.
Was it always this way?
Or perhaps we never noticed.

Has the TV screen, movie theatres
and popular magazines
made it more obvious than ever
how cruel we are to each other?

A Child was born in a nearby country
in a poor and lowly Jewish village
not so long ago,   but only seems so.
A Child He was and a Child He is today.

The irony of ironies to find
that the salvation of my mind
is learning to trust again
with the trust of a little child.

With all my years, there
is but one thing
I have come to know for sure:
the child in me cries
out in desperation
for the trust that I once knew
in childhood.

Quiet desperation turns
suddenly to joy
when I look upon the Child.
world's madness no
longer seems so mad
whenever I contemplate Him.

For, after all, if God chose to
become a little child and more like me
to conquer madness,
who am I, then to question the
world's craziness?

The Creator becomes the creature:
what greater madness can there be?!
I lovingly embrace and draw it to me,
the more to become like Him.

... IN CHAOS

Continued

Joy in the midst of insanity,
you say?
How else explain the way
I pray to a God
who poses as an infant
lying in His Mother's arms?

The grand contradiction it seems
is that I am born only to learn to die:
a life-long study in which my grades
are barely passing.

What is dying
if it is not learning to live
with the upsidedownness
of it all?

There is no explaining
the reason for the Beginning
without understanding the
ending to my life.
I live to die and die to live.

How strange it must seem to you
and all who find it hard to fathom
the Child in the soiled crib,
in the ancient
town of Nazareth.

If I'm to make any sense
out of all the chaos
that surrounds me,
I must again become...

...a little child.

Mother of

Mary, you deserve
so much more
from life than this.

Sorrow is your middle name:
Mother of sorrows,
Sorrowful Mother.

"Why me? Why me, Lord?
Yet, I accept this sorrow
you have laid upon me."

"Abandoned by my Son,
alone, I am resigned
to my sorrow."

The torment of your soul, Mary,
is beyond tears; it is cast
in darkness,
the emptiness of an aching,
broken heart.

There are no tears left in you.
Your sadness is unspoken,
caring only for your
tortured Son.

Beautiful, kind and tender
young and gentle are you,
Mother of your only Son.

Sorrows

I wish that I could weep
for you in your deep sorrow;
but tears won't come.

You move me to an anguish akin to pity
for myself and others of my kind,
who know not the depths of the
sorrow in your heart.

I cannot look upon your eyes
without feeling sadness
in my heart for you.

I wish that I could touch
your tearless eyes
and wipe away your sadness.

How much sorrow
You have known
in such short a life!

I love you,
Mother of deep sorrow,
and thank you,
for the grace to share
even the tiniest fragment
of your deep sorrow.

No greater sorrow
than the one you bear for your Son.
You bear it all, dear Mother, for Him—
and for me.

33

Warmed By Your Love

March winds find their likeness
in pent up feelings
of deep-down,
hard-rock emptiness.

Fiery, angry, howling
at the nothingness
sent to plague my soul
in its freeze-dried
loneliness.

Demon-like, frenzied
in its sinfulness,
spreads its lies
to ensure my eternal
forgetfulness.

However chilling
its willfulness,
my spirit remains
warmed in your
unfailing helpfulness.

34

Come Holy Breath

Come Holy Breath,
fill my heart
with the fire
of your love.

Holy Breath,
you are God-artist
of my soul;
you are gentle,
sweetness,
kind and loving.

Your kisses
cover my
entire being;
you enter my
body and soul
like a lover,
filling me,
caressing me,
lifting me
to heights
unimaginable.

You are grace itself,
leading me
to passion and love
for the Father and Son.

Words on paper
cannot describe
the infinite love
with which you fill
my heart and soul.

Lover never was
who loved so;
love never found
that tasted so.

35

MY FEARS

My fears
are my innermost self,

signaling awareness of love lost
in trial, finding joy and happiness
in the depths of discovering self.

Fear is a prelude to timeless vision,
open to pictures of timeless beauty…

… finding the soul
in love with itself
in the image of its God.

WHITHER SORROW

Heavenbent is stealth
finding its way to the stars
and seeing no one standing
there empty-handed.

Vacuuming the skies with a broom lets me fill my nights
with boredom, knowing full well that words come and go,
emptying themselves of all that is true and beautiful.

Smiles are not easily purchased
when one is filled with despair.
Tears sell like hotcakes grilled on open flames.

I teeter on the edge of a sidewalk,
moving along the main streets of hell,
while all else seems so distant and cold-like.

And yet, sounds of distant voices cry out
like a child's screams in the middle of the night:
"Come to me, Oh mother earth, sun and moon."

I ask mother earth to heal the wounds of my heart.
and fold my hands in deepest supplication.
I wish not to live and die a lonely beggar.

I ask only for room to breathe and sigh
and whisper that I am not too human to plead
when everyone sees themselves in me.

My tears turn suddenly into rivers of joy;
strange, unparalleled twists of irony
that make of my pain exquisite joy and ecstasy.

The salt taste of my tears turns into honey, caressing the pallet of my soul with tenderness.

37

The Shaman's Secret

Compassionate
in a world of sorrows,
her soul is seared
with the burdens and trials
of others who weep and mourn.

She carries
and cares for earth's children.
In her heart she weeps for
their losses and failures and trials.

On her face she wears only a smile,
her eyes resplendent with light.
in her heart burns
a fire of passion and love.

The soul of a Shaman she carries within,
from her hands and her fingers
there radiates heat,
whose healing is felt
with the power of the sun.

Whomever she touches along the way
remembers her kindness
and gentleness curing their illness
of mind and heart and soul.

The source of her power
she keeps hidden and safe;
protected from those who would steal it away:
nourished and fed from the Fountain of Love.

To live life again
is her fondest wish,
for the healing and caring
can never end.

Generations will know her
in the touch of her hands.
Trees stand as sentinels
to her remembrance.

Rivers empty into oceans of her caring.
Winters turn Spring into flowers
reminding us all of her beauty.

A healer, a creatrix, she stands alone
as one who gives witness
to God's love for us.
my Shaman, Mary, soul-mate forever.

YOUNG LOVE

My son, my son,
you cry the cry
of children down the ages:

I wish to be a man, yet
young remain
and rewrite all life's pages.

Nowhere to go,
as friends outgrow their toys.
They seem like men,
and yet they act as boys.

The time has quickly come
when love outshines the cares;
when boyhood dreams
seem distant as the stars

She touched your soul
with winsome awkwardness;
and you respond
with manly helplessness.

There was a time
when love was a far-off thing;
the time has now come
when you hear your heart sing.

You play the tune
with fingers on the strings,
and songs come forth
with angel-feathered wings.

39

A WORK OF ART

No poem, song, painting, or work of art
that endures the test of time
is ever created without tears.

Tears of joy or anguish often
accompany them,
since birth is never predictable
or devoid of any emotion.

The soul of a work of art
is like a human soul -
it outlives its creator.

It comes into this world
kicking and screaming,
pulsing with the blood of
its progenitor.

For it to live, the artist
cuts the cord,
and allows it to inhabit
its own space and time.

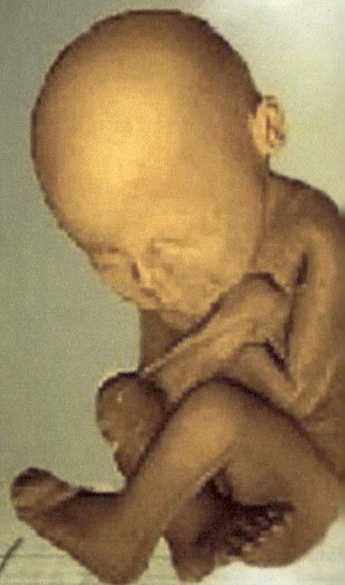

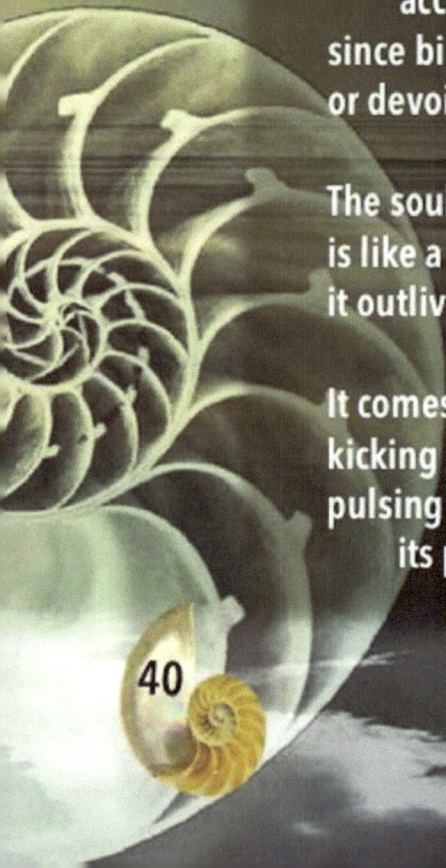

WIND WHIRL

To love once
is to die a
thousand times.

And in loving death, the heart
seeks to find itself
in the ashes of its ecstasy.

Burning and burning and burning
knows only the flames of
human revelation.

I'm open to a world in which
the winds whirl the fire
about legs and arms and thawing heart.

The fire breeds a strange death to all that is not holy and divine, and human in love.

41

PRODIGAL SELF

As a prodigal I discover
the fatherhood of my soul
wrested from the trough
of self-pity.

I conceive a child
new born in ecstasy,
fulfilling my dreams
in numbered days.

Silence reclaims its birthright
and tears wash away
sins of forgetfulness…

Remembered only is the joy
of finding renewal
in the arms of my beloved.

NARCISSUS OF THE SOUL

My soul looks deep into itself
and falls in love
with what it sees.

Sight is given to an eternity of todays,
open vistas of the self longing for redemption
and finding only love.

Warmth is peace and mild comfort in a newness,
loveliness adorned, fragrance of the stars,
earth-bent for mere mortality in an everlasting joyfulness.

Eye cannot see,
nor ear hear, nor tongue taste
the sheer beauty of the soul in
love with itself.

Nowhere beleaguered
more than in the struggle
to find oneself
in the trees and forests
of the mind.

**Discovery comes
in a clear, silent
pool of water
reflecting back the
image of self, in love.**

WUTHERING

Winter returns with a vengeance
and darkness flirts with gray shadows
from dawn to dusk, dulling my senses
and lulling me quietly to sleep.

The geese return honking their way
into my wakefulness,
reminding me of frozen ponds
and fish hibernating
deep within cold waters of my soul.

Ice forms upon branches of maples,
standing tall and headstrong against the cold.
The icy winds tease the magnolias
into thinking winter is past,
and rage even more.

Crisp air interrupted by wisps of smoke
cascading down from chimneys,
surrounded by birds, huddling to keep warm,
like the homeless around barrels of fire
in the back alleys of our cities and towns.

The rhythm of the cold days beats relentlessly
as fires burn and turn to ashes and burn again,
until warmth and cold reverse themselves,
and I am fooled into thinking
that the season is forever.

44

WUTHERING
Continued

Cruel winds beat against the
windows of my soul,
reminding me of my mortality.
I escape beneath the covers of my bed,
seeking protection
from the chills of daily existence.

If I could sleep the winter through,
and awaken only to hear the robins
frolicking in the fresh spring grass,
I would gladly live half a life
and donate the other half to polar bears,
and others who worship mother snow.

And hearing my groans,
the hoary teacher reminds me
that winter is a season of rest,
readying my soul for the
rebirth of spring,
and the dizzying heights of summer.

**The season of dead leaves
and frost-bitten fingers is a quiet teacher,
patiently withstanding my complaints.**

45

THE FAMILY PHOTO ALBUM

Yes, it is only human no to want to give up what you believe you possess.

But whose is the possession? "Surely not yours," says the Lord. "For I made your children for Myself, to forever reside in Me. Yours, for the moment - mine, for eternity."
As I turn the pages of the photo albums, I am torn between happy and sad.

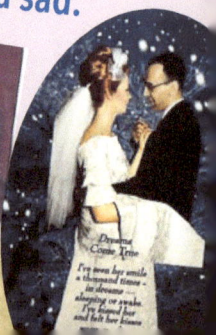

Sad to realize that time has gone by as quickly as the rising and setting of the sun. Happy to know their spirits still mix with their bodies and walk the earth beside me.

Older, and grown away but not so far that time and distance will not allow their voices to embrace me in fondness, remembering the good times as well as the bad.

Bittersweet are memories of times past and at times I felt that I could do without them.

Wouldn't I be better off, I ask, if I had lost my memory? If so, I would not hurt as much.

Oh but then, what would there be to cherish and to laugh at in the twilight of my living?

Memories are but the foodstuff souls subsist upon, devouring each with a deep hunger.

Without them life would be but a tunnel of forgotten pasts, with no beginning or no end.

I welcome the tears I wash away with the turn of the page of the photo album.

Faces of my ever-young children smiling out at me, reminding me that time indeed has not passed, and that their love is ever in the present.

"There is only NOW in our love for you," their smiles wish to say,

"and now will be forever, wherever you or we may be."

47

BREATH OF GOD, THE ADVOCATE

The Holy Breath
is not a ghost,
a phantom,
nor a chimera.

The Holy Breath is a Person,
the Third Person of
of the Blessed Trinity.

The Holy Breath
lives within me,
and I in the Holy Breath.

We are one with each other.
I live, not I,
but the Holy Breath lives in me.

I live in the Holy Breath;
and all grace in me
comes from
the Holy Breath
of God.

The Holy Breath
moves me,
teaches me
how to live.

And loving thus,
I come to love
the Infinite.

And I am able to
love all those
who dwell
within God,
as I come to
love myself.

www.ingramcontent.com/pod-product-compliance
Lightning Source LLC
LaVergne TN
LVHW072053070426
835508LV00002B/71